CREATING FUNNY COMICS

MORENO CHIACCHIERA

PowerKiDS
press

NEW YORK

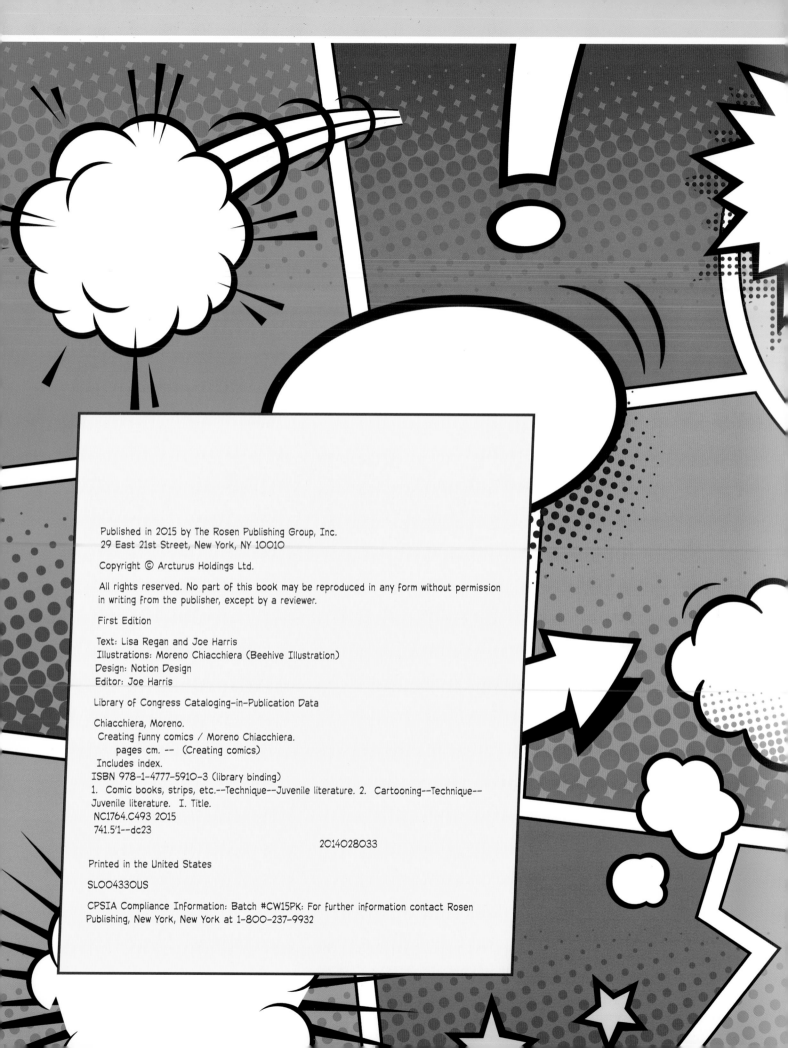

Published in 2015 by The Rosen Publishing Group, Inc.
29 East 21st Street, New York, NY 10010

First Edition

Text: Lisa Regan and Joe Harris
Illustrations: Moreno Chiacchiera (Beehive Illustration)
Design: Notion Design
Editor: Joe Harris

Library of Congress Cataloging-in-Publication Data

Chiacchiera, Moreno.
  Creating funny comics / Moreno Chiacchiera.
      pages cm. -- (Creating comics)
  Includes index.
  ISBN 978-1-4777-5910-3 (library binding)
  1. Comic books, strips, etc.--Technique--Juvenile literature. 2. Cartooning--Technique--Juvenile literature. I. Title.
  NC1764.C493 2015
  741.5'1--dc23

                                2014028033

Printed in the United States

SL004330US

CPSIA Compliance Information: Batch #CW15PK: For further information contact Rosen Publishing, New York, New York at 1-800-237-9932

CONTENTS

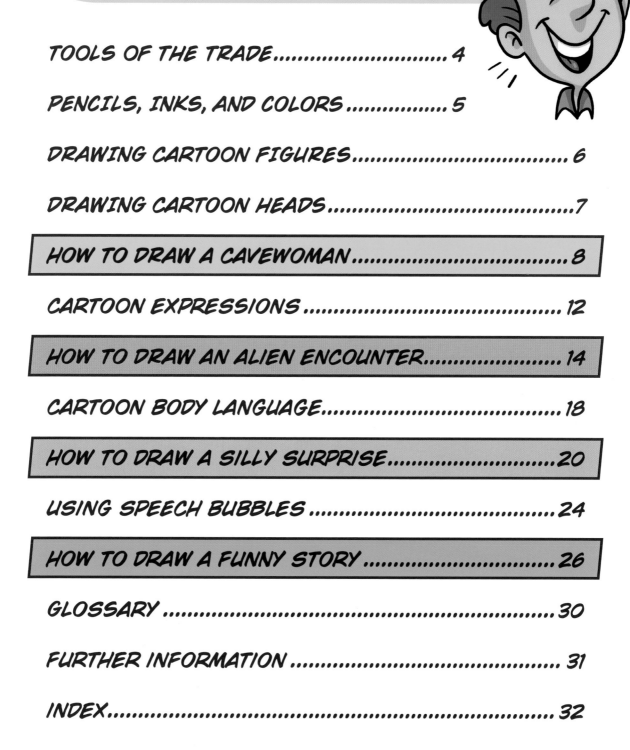

TOOLS OF THE TRADE

THE GREAT THING ABOUT DRAWING FUNNY COMICS IS THAT YOU DON'T NEED EXPENSIVE EQUIPMENT TO GET STARTED. JUST GRAB THE ITEMS BELOW, AND YOU'RE READY TO GO!

PENCILS

Soft (B, 2B) pencils are great for drawing loosely and are easy to erase. Fine point pencils are handy for adding detail.

ERASERS

A kneaded eraser molds to shape, so you can use it to remove pencil from tiny areas. Keep a clean, square-edged eraser to hand, too.

PENS

An artist's pens are his or her most precious tools! Gather a selection with different tips for varying the thickness of your line work.

FINE LINE AND BRUSH PENS

Fine line pens are excellent for small areas of detail. Brush pens are perfect for varying your line weight or shading large areas.

PENCILS, INKS, AND COLORS

THERE ARE FOUR MAIN STAGES IN THE DRAWING PROCESS. IF YOU FOLLOW THIS METHOD, IT WILL SAVE YOU FROM FINDING BASIC MISTAKES WHEN IT IS TOO LATE TO FIX THEM!

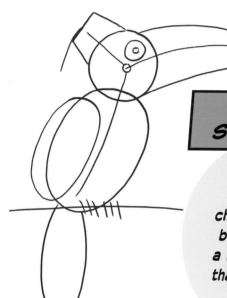

ROUGH SKETCHES

Each of the crazy characters in this book starts with a basic framework that is made up of simple outline shapes.

TIGHT SKETCHES

When you are happy with the basic frame, you can tighten it up with firm pencil strokes and add in some shading.

INKS

Ink over your best pencil lines. Then erase your rough sketch. Now you're ready for the final stage of the process!

COLORS

It's fun to color your cartoons. You can use shading and highlights to make them feel three-dimensional.

DRAWING CARTOON FIGURES

YOU CAN HAVE A LOT OF FUN PLAYING AROUND WITH THE BODY SHAPES OF YOUR FUNNY CHARACTERS. HOWEVER, WHEN YOU ARE DRAWING A COMIC, YOU WILL NEED TO MAKE SURE THAT THEY STAY THE SAME FROM ONE PANEL TO THE NEXT.

SLIM JIM

This man looks incredibly skinny because he has narrow shoulders and a tubelike torso. His head is just as wide as his body! His arms are the correct length, reaching to midthigh height.

COUCH POTATO

This man has been blown up like a balloon. His head and body both bulge at the bottom. His legs are so short, they have virtually disappeared. His arms only just reach past his waist.

BEANPOLE

Everything about this girl looks stretched! Her neck is long and her body is a thin, curved line. Her big feet make her arms and legs look even more thin and spindly!

EGGHEAD

This lady's body is tiny compared to her huge head. She also has large eyes behind her glasses. This is all part of a cartoon's jokey sense of reality. She is brainy, so she must have a huge brain!

DRAWING CARTOON HEADS

IN A FUNNY CARTOON STORY, YOU SHOULD GIVE YOUR CHARACTERS SILLY, EXAGGERATED FACIAL FEATURES. BUT WHICH FEATURES SHOULD YOU EXAGGERATE?

FEELING NOSY

This character's comedy schnoz is huge and rounded. Male cartoon characters tend to have larger noses than female ones.

In profile, it's easy to see how exaggerated the nose is. It's nearly the width of the head!

MAD HAIR DAY

Hairstyles can help to convey a character's personality and age. This big, curly style says "mom"!

A sideways view shows her turned-up nose, enormous eyes, and pursed lips.

PUPPY POWER

The dog's drooping tongue, close-set eyes, and wide smile all add up to give him a goofy look.

From the side, his whole muzzle area sticks out—not just his nose.

HOW TO DRAW
A CAVEWOMAN

MEET STONE-AGE SHIRLEY, A NO-NONSENSE CAVEWOMAN WITH A HEARTY APPETITE. SHE'S GOING CLUBBING IN A VERY LITERAL SENSE! WHEN THEY SEE HER COMING, DINOSAURS TURN AND RUN IN TERROR. IF YOU ENJOY DRAWING HER, WHY NOT GIVE HER A PREHISTORIC PAL?

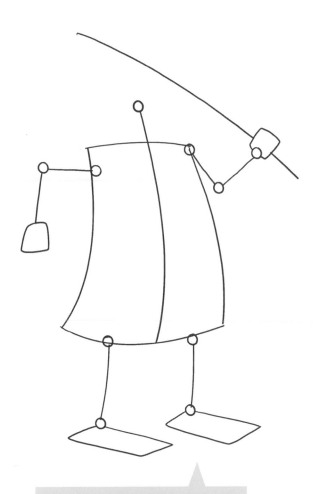

1 Start with a curved rectangle for the body. Sketch where her legs and arms will be. Add a line for the club.

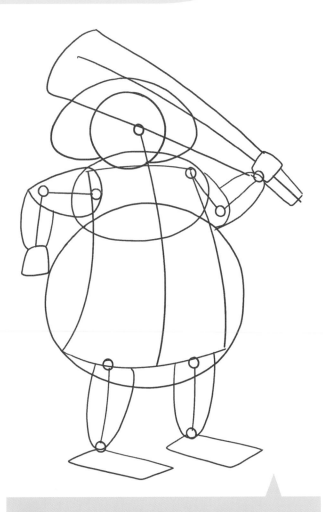

2 Fill out the body with circles and ovals. Notice how she has no knees! This makes her look shorter and fatter. Add her head and a rough outline for her hair.

3 Work up the outline of her body, clothed in a simple tunic. Sketch in her fingers and toes. Some cartoonists prefer to draw hands with only three fingers, but there is room here for a full hand. Erase your guide lines, and add her facial features.

4 Now you can add the finer details to her face and hair. Give her a wild look, with untamed hair and big pupils. Use small lines to show the bumps on her elbows and ankles. Sketch some lines and swirls on the club to make it look wooden.

5 It's time to ink in the outline of your cavewoman! You can see just how simple and clean the lines of a cartoon should be. There is very little detail, just a bold shape based around smooth curves. Simple shapes will be the basis of all your characters.

6 The uncomplicated shape allows you to have fun when you're coloring in. Shirley is modeling the latest in animal print daywear! Notice how the shading and highlights on her face, hair, and stomach make her look three-dimensional.

CARTOON EXPRESSIONS

YOUR BEST TOOL WHEN IT COMES TO DRAWING EXPRESSIONS IS A MIRROR. YOU MAY FEEL A BIT SILLY MAKING FACES AT YOURSELF, BUT IT'S A TECHNIQUE THAT MANY PROFESSIONAL CARTOONISTS USE!

HAPPY

Woo-hoo! Raised eyebrows, upward-curving closed eyes, and a huge open grin show how happy this fella is right now.

SAD

Sigh! This glum guy has drooping eyes and a downturned mouth. His eyebrows are raised in the middle.

ANGRY

Grr! Use gritted teeth and reddened cheeks to show that your character is fuming. Lowered eyebrows help as well.

CONFUSED

Huh? Large, opened-up eyes and a small, circular mouth show this girl doesn't get it. Her eyebrows are raised, too.

SCARED

Yikes! Gritted teeth, wide eyes, high eyebrows, and beads of sweat show us that this character is terrified!

EMBARRASSED

Shucks! Blushing is a sure sign of embarrassment, with a wide, shut mouth to prevent anything else from slipping out in shame.

WORRIED

Oh no, something's up! This girl is sweating and biting her lip. Her eyebrows are raised and her eyes are big and round. She is blushing, though not as much as her friend on the left.

SURPRISED

Eek! The easiest way to show shock is to make the eyes and mouth round and open, with the hair standing on end.

BORED

SNEAKY

Teehee! Hunched shoulders and narrowed eyes show this dude is up to no good. His sly grin and furrowed brow add to the effect.

Zzz ... Half-closed eyes and small "daydream bubbles" tell you this guy is sleepy. His mouth is closed and downturned, pushed up at the corner by his hand.

AN ALIEN ENCOUNTER

TO CREATE A HUMOROUS COMIC STORY, YOU WILL NEED MORE THAN ONE CHARACTER. CAPTAIN INTREPID MAY BE A BRAVE SPACE EXPLORER, BUT HE'S NOT THAT BRIGHT. WHILE HE'S LAUGHING AT A LITTLE ALIEN, SOMETHING ELSE HAS CREPT UP ON HIM ...

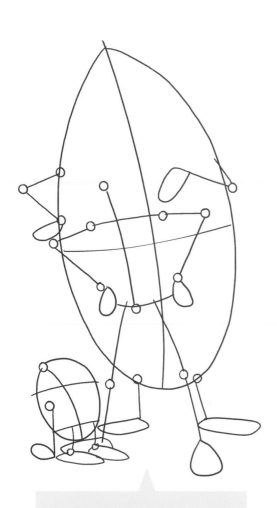

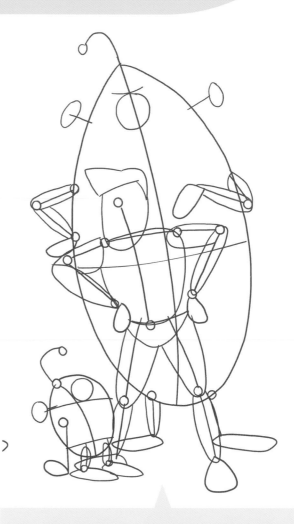

1 Sketch outlines for all three shapes to make sure they're in proportion and in the right place in relation to each other.

2 Concentrate on one character at a time. Flesh out the hero's body with ovals, and add the shape of his head. Now add the arms, ears, and antennae of your alien creations.

3 Have fun designing a costume for your main man. Most space heroes shop at the same store, and wear belts and boots over their tight-fitting suits. Play around with different expressions on the three faces.

4 These two aliens are from the same planet, so they both have similar markings. The big beastie needs a frown and teeth, while the little fella is much less scary. Make your hero look big and strong with a defined chest and abs.

5 Erase any leftover guides, and ink in the final lines with firm, thin strokes. Keep it simple, with tiny lines to show the knees and elbows. A few extra movement and expression lines and small beads of sweat help to tell the funny story.

6 When you're creating creatures from your imagination, you can use any colors that you like. Notice how each eye has a small white highlight, and the shading is a darker tone than the main body colors. Add paler shades for highlights.

CARTOON BODY LANGUAGE

CARTOONS ARE ALL ABOUT EXAGGERATION. IF YOU USE REALISTIC POSES IN A FUNNY COMIC, THEY WILL LOOK VERY STATIC! CRAZY, OVER-THE-TOP POSES ARE MUCH MORE FUN.

REALISTIC RUNNING

Real people run with bent limbs and a very slight forward-leaning stance.

REALISTIC SURPRISE

Real people pull back in shock and lift their arms to protect their faces. They may jump very slightly.

CARTOON SURPRISE

Not so in cartoons. These guys leap high in the air, hair on end, arms outstretched, and tongue hanging out. Not realistic but much funnier!

CARTOON RUNNING

Cartoon runners lift their arms and legs high and stick their heads forward. This fellow's big nose might help him cross the line first, too!

A REALISTIC PUNCH

Oof! Take that! Real boxers lean into a punch and recoil slightly if they're on the receiving end of the blow.

A CARTOON PUNCH

Even being hit in the face can be made funny in a cartoon. Everything is exaggerated, from the body shapes to the movements involved. One guy is superskinny, and the other is bulked up.

A SILLY SURPRISE

TRICK OR TREAT! WHO KNOWS WHAT HORRORS ARE LURKING ON HALLOWEEN? DRACULA CERTAINLY WASN'T EXPECTING TO COME FACE TO FACE WITH THIS CUTE KID WANTING CANDY! HE'S FRIGHTENED TO DEATH, IF THAT'S EVEN POSSIBLE FOR A VAMPIRE.

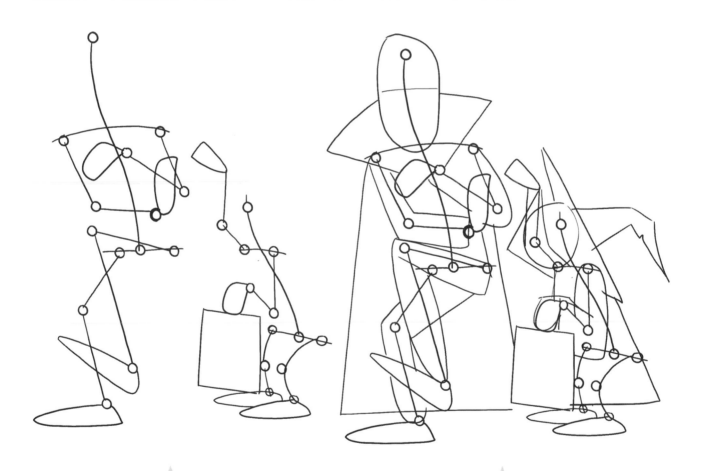

1 The positions here are quite tricky, so take your time getting them right. Dracula is hunched, even though he is tall.

2 Sketch a long oval for Dracula's face and a circle for the small girl's head. Add the outline of their clothes, and then flesh out the arms and legs in front.

3 Draw the features on both faces. Dracula should have a pointed nose and ears, while the girl has round, cute features. Erase your guide lines, and make sure the clothes are the way you want them to be. Don't forget the hair standing on end!

4 Have fun with the details, such as the girl's candy bag and Halloween costume. Her hat is overly bent, and her cloak has patches on it. Use small lines to add definition to Dracula's cape and collar. You can also add movement marks around his body to show how he's feeling.

5 Inking in a black-clad character is tricky. You will need to leave white lines in place of your usual black lines, to show the outline shape. See how Dracula's legs, arms, and cape all have white edges and are filled in with solid black?

6 Use the same technique if you're coloring your picture, with blue-gray lines instead of white. Color helps to highlight tiny details, such as the girl's freckles and the pink of Dracula's eyes and the inside of his mouth, showing off his pointed fangs.

USING SPEECH BUBBLES

COMIC STORIES ARE MADE UP OF PICTURES AND WORDS. YOU SHOULD MAKE SURE THEY WORK IN HARMONY! HERE ARE SOME HANDY DOS AND DON'TS TO REMEMBER WHEN YOU'RE USING SPEECH BUBBLES.

LOOK AT WHERE YOU'RE POINTING

Always point the speech bubble toward a character's mouth. It doesn't have to actually touch the mouth—it just needs to point in that general direction.

BUBBLE BLOCKING

Think carefully about where you will position your speech bubbles when you are planning your cartoon. If you don't leave room in the panel for a speech bubble, you will ruin your artwork.

READING LEFT TO RIGHT

We usually read from left to right. Think about who is speaking first. It's a good idea to put the first speaker on the left side of a caption.

TOO MUCH INFORMATION

Don't try to cram too many words into a single caption! It will look plain wrong.

A FUNNY STORY

DRAWING AND WRITING A CARTOON STORY TAKES CAREFUL PLANNING. THE STORY NEEDS TO FIT INTO THE SPACE YOU HAVE AND PROGRESS DOWN THE PAGE. EACH PIECE OF ACTION TAKES PLACE IN A "PANEL" OR "CELL"—A RECTANGULAR BOX CONTAINING CHARACTERS AND SPEECH.

1 Write your story in five or six sentences. Then divide your page into the same number of panels. Loosely sketch the characters in each one. Vary the position of your "camera" from panel to panel. Draw in the speech bubbles, but resist adding detail until the next stage.

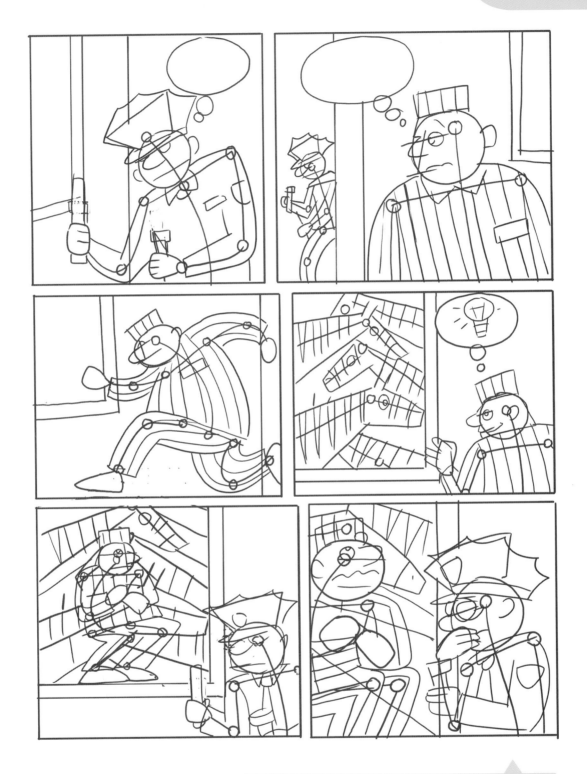

2 Now you can start to flesh things out. Our story is about a
cop and the robber he's chasing in an art gallery. You may find
that it helps to draw the main characters on a separate piece of
paper, so that you can refer back to a correct version of them.

3 When you've taken the pencils to the most detailed stage and are satisfied with all of the panels, start using inks. You won't often use a ruler when drawing cartoons, but it's a good idea to use one for drawing the outlines of panels.

4 The fastest way to color a multipanel story is to fill in one character in all the panels, then the other, then the backgrounds. Avoid making the backgrounds too bright, since you will want your characters to stand out.

GLOSSARY

CAPTION (KAP-shuhn)
A piece of text that helps tell your story.

CELL (SEL)
A single rectangle that makes up part of your comic strip (see also PANEL).

CONSISTENT (kuhn-SIS-tent)
The same the whole way through.

EXAGGERATED
(ehg-ZAJ-juhr-ray-tehd)
Made larger so that it is no longer realistic.

EXPRESSION (eks-PREH-shuhn)
The look on a character's face that shows their feelings.

HIGHLIGHTS (HY-lytz)
The palest parts of a drawing that show where the light falls.

PANEL (PAN-nuhl)
A single rectangle that makes up a part of your comic strip (see also CELL).

POSTURE (PAHS-chur)
The position of a figure.

PROPORTION (pruh-POHR-shuhn)
The size of body parts in relation to each other.

SHADING (SHAY-ding)
The darker parts of a drawing that show shadows or where the light cannot reach.

SKETCH (SKECH)
A rough drawing for practice or to make neater later on.

FURTHER INFORMATION

FURTHER READING

Hart, Christopher. *Cartooning: The Ultimate Character Design Book.* New York: Christopher Hart Books, 2008.

Roche, Art. *Art for Kids: Cartooning: The Only Cartooning Book You'll Ever Need to Be the Artist You've Always Wanted to Be.* New York: Sterling Publishing, 2010.

Yomtov, Nel. *How to Write a Comic Book.* North Mankato, MN: Cherry Lake Publishing, 2013.

WEBSITES

Due to the changing nature of internet links, PowerKids Press has developed an online list of sites related to the subject of this book. This site is updated regularly. Please use this link to access the list:

www.powerkidslinks.com/cc/funny

INDEX